How To Be A

GREAT STUDENT LEADER

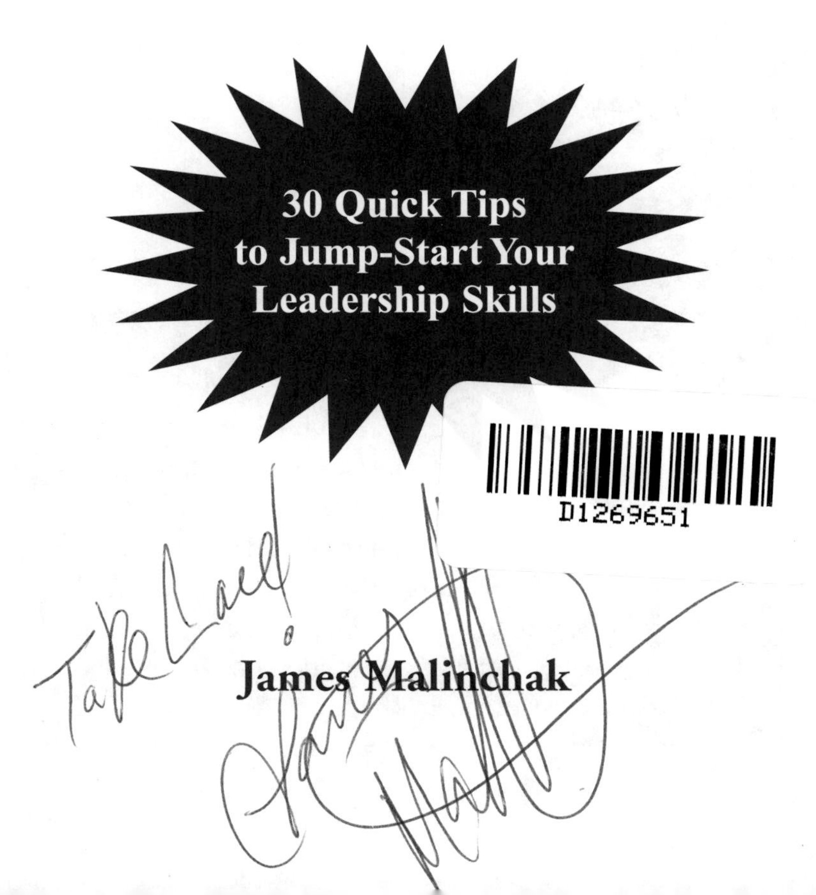

James Malinchak

Published by Positive Publishing

Printed in the United States of America

ISBN 0-9646924-4-9

Warning - Disclaimer

The purpose of this book is to educate and entertain. The authors or publisher does not guarantee that anyone following the techniques, suggestions, tips, ideas, or strategies will become successful. The authors and publisher shall have neither liability or responsibility to anyone with respect to any loss or damage caused, or alleged to be caused, directly or indirectly by the information contained in this book.

Speaking Engagements

James Malinchak is recognized worldwide as one of the top motivational speakers for students. He was voted College Speaker of the Year by Campus Activities magazine and the Association for the Promotion of Campus Activities (APCA). James has delivered his motivational messages at more than 1,500 youth events, colleges and conferences worldwide.

James is the author of ten books including the top-sellers, *From College to the Real World* and *Teenagers Tips for Success*. He is a Contributing Author to, and serves as an Associate Editor for, the #1 Best-selling book series *Chicken Soup for the Soul®*. James is also a Contributing Editor for *Chicken Soup for the College Soul®* and is published in *Chicken Soup for the Teenage Soul®*.

To Check Speaking Availability, Contact:

JamesMal@aol.com
1-888-793-1196
www.Malinchak.com

Also By James Malinchak

From College to the Real World:
Street-Smart Strategies for Landing Your Dream Job and Creating a Successful Future

Teenagers Tips for Success:
Create a Future, Achieve Your Dreams and Become Very Successful

Success Starts With Attitude:
50 Ways to Refuel, Recharge and Reenergize Yourself in Business and Life

How to Be A Master Networker:
7 Secrets for Getting What You Want Through Who You Know (Co-Authored with Joe Martin)

Success Starts With Attitude
(Audio CD) - James Malinchak Live!

For a complete catalog of James Malinchak's books, audio and video success products, contact:

James Malinchak International
JamesMal@aol.com
www.Malinchak.com
1-888-793-1196

MESSAGE TO YOU!

Congratulations!

I'm so proud of you for making the great decision to be a student leader. You have an incredible opportunity to make a positive difference in the lives of other students. This is a tremendous responsibility and I admire you for accepting the role.

I wanted to write a quick and simple guide that would make your job a little easier. You'll notice one important fact about this book.....it's short!

Why? Because I understand that you're busy with many other school and personal activities. I don't believe that a book is better simply because there's more written in it.

I wanted to create a simple, easy-to-read book that you could read in 20-30 minutes that would stimulate your thinking. I wanted this book to be short and to the point so you'll finish it.

The tips in this book are just that—tips. These are quick tips that you will read and immediately be able to apply to better lead yourself and other students.

Again, congratulations on accepting your leadership role. I truly admire you for that great decision and wish you and your organization nothing but continued success!

-James Malinchak

GREAT

LEADER

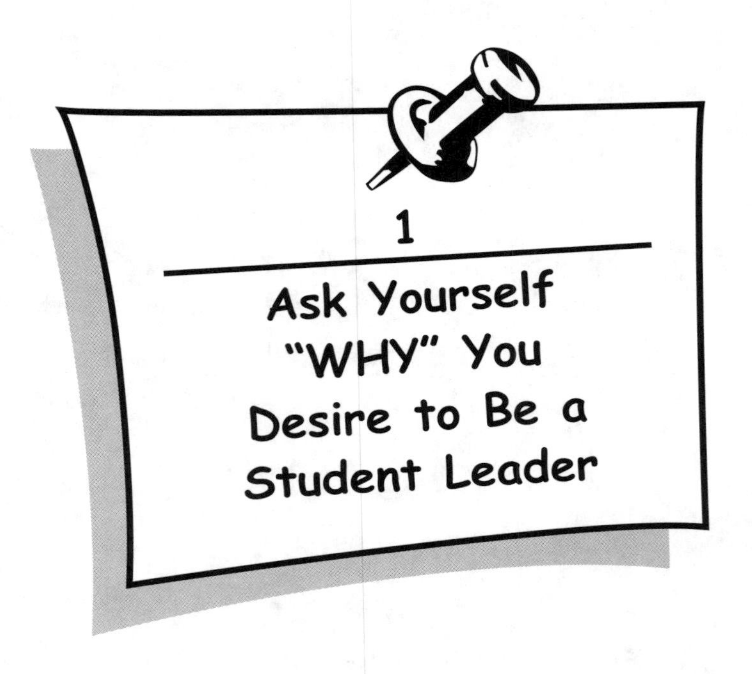

1
Ask Yourself "WHY" You Desire to Be a Student Leader

My good friend, Professor Joe Martin, once taught me one of the most important lessons for becoming a successful leader. He said it all starts with developing a strong "why" statement.

Without a strong statement as to "why" you desire to be a student leader, you will lack vision, purpose and desire.

Quick Action Step

Write a "why" statement clearly explaining the reason you desire to be a student leader.

GREAT

LEADER

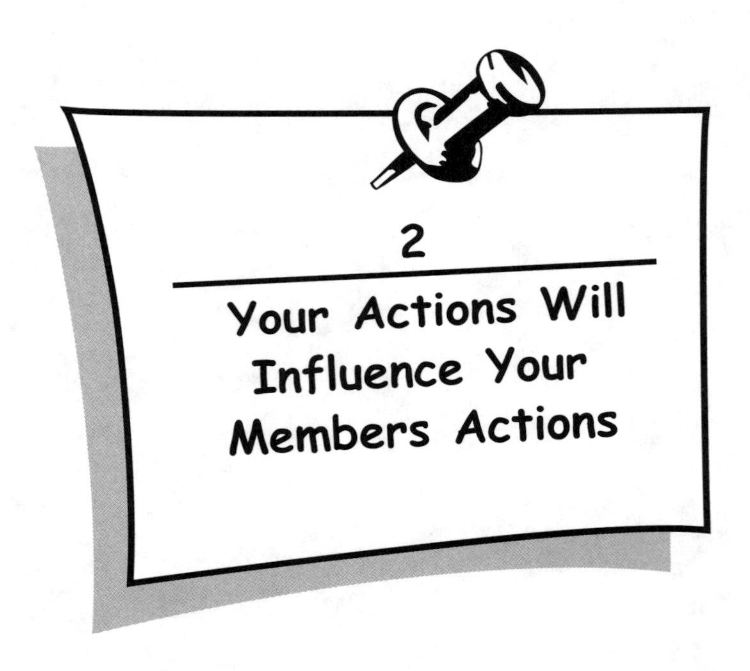

2 Your Actions Will Influence Your Members Actions

Those within your group watch you more than you think and their actions will mirror YOUR actions.

If YOU, as a leader, choose:

...not to arrive at meetings on time
...not to finish your part of the project
...not to treat others in a correct manner

Then, don't be surprised if those you are leading have similar actions. Why? Because you lead more by example than words.

Quick Action Step

List three actions YOU can immediately improve to improve the actions of those you are leading.

GREAT

LEADER

3 Respect All Suggestions and Ideas

Unfortunately, many student leaders don't positively reinforce certain suggestions and ideas offered by group members. Often the reason is the suggestions or ideas may seem different or unusual.

As a student leader, it's critically important to respect all suggestions and ideas while being open-minded to the possibility of implementing them. Just because certain suggestions or ideas may seem different or unusual doesn't mean they will not benefit the organization.

Quick Action Step

List two suggestions or ideas that one of your group members recently offered that you may have disregarded because they seemed different or unusual. Then, seriously think about how you may be able to use them to benefit your group.

GREAT

LEADER

I have never met one person, especially someone who is a member of a group, who doesn't have the desire to receive encouragement and praise.

To get more positive production out of those you are leading, look for ways to encourage, rather than discourage. Too many leaders tend to focus on the negative rather than the positive. In every situation and with every individual, YOU can choose to find two or three reasons to criticize a person or two to three reasons to praise that person.

Quick Action Step

List one or two ways you have recently criticized a group member. Then, list how you can turn that criticism into positive, uplifting encouragement and praise.

GREAT

LEADER

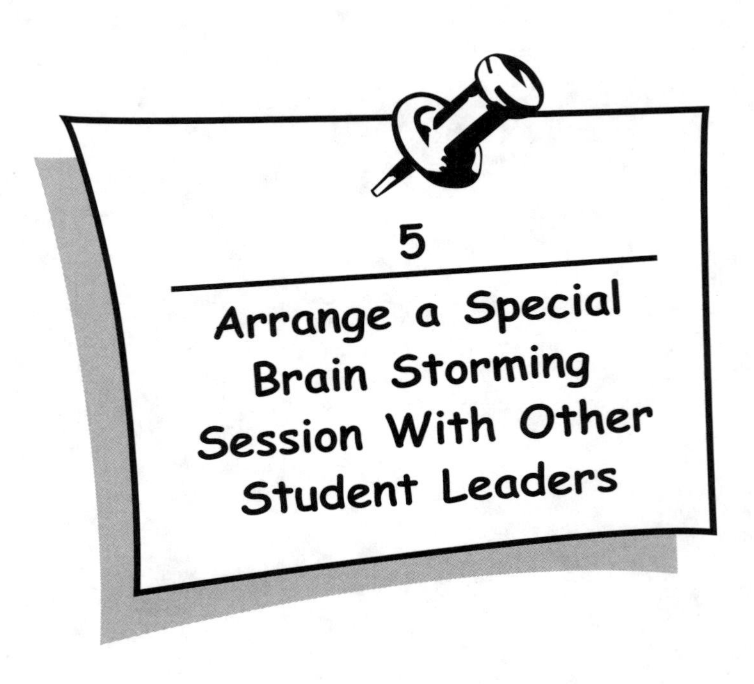

5

Arrange a Special Brain Storming Session With Other Student Leaders

One of the most powrful ways to learn new ideas, tips and strategies for becoming a better leader is to organize a special brain storming session with other student leaders.

Take the initiative to set a date and time for all student club and organization leaders to meet to exchange ideas. Ask each student leader to present their three best ideas for creating enthusiasm and accomplishing their group objectives.

Also, have each student leader present their biggest challenge or problem and have everyone offer creative suggestions to help that particular student leader. You will be amazed at the incredible ideas and solutions this brain storming session will produce.

Quick Action Step

List the date and time of the first special brain storming session you WILL organize. Then, do it!

GREAT

LEADER

Let me ask you a question. Have you ever received a hand written thank you note thanking you for something you've done? Of course you have. How did it make you feel? Probably pretty good. You probably said to yourself, "Wow! He/she really appreciates what I did." I'll bet receiving the note made you want to do even more to help the person who wrote you the note. It's human nature. The same is true for your group members. Start writing them thank you notes and watch their performance soar to new levels.

Quick Action Step

List all of your group members then list a reason to thank each of them. Purchase an inexpensive package of thank you notes and write one to each group member...ASAP! Then, write them often!

GREAT

LEADER

7
Look for Solutions for Overcoming Challenges

It's inevitable that your group will encounter various challenges while pursuing your organizational goals. As these challenges present themselves, it's easy for group members to fall into the trap of giving up. One of your roles as a student leader is to keep group members motivated to keep plugging along. One of the easiest ways to accomplish this is by getting everyone to focus on solutions, not excuses.

"If you focus on the excuses why you can't, you'll never find the solutions for how you can!"

Quick Action Step

List the two primary challenges facing your group and two solutions for overcoming these challenges. Then, get your group members to focus on these solutions and ask them for ideas for other possible solutions.

GREAT

LEADER

8

Delegate Certain Tasks to Group Members

Many student leaders don't understand the importance of delegating certain tasks to group members. Why is it important as a student leader to delegate? Two primary reasons: 1). Delegating certain tasks will give you more free time. As a leader you have many responsibilities associated with your position and can't possibly handle every task associated with group projects; and 2). Delegating certain tasks will create a bond with your members because you are indirectly telling them that you value and trust their opinions, ideas and ability.

Quick Action Step

List five or more tasks you've been working on that you WILL immediately delegate to group members.

GREAT

LEADER

9

How to Determine Which Task Gets Delegated to Which Group Member

It's one thing to recommend that you delegate certain tasks to group members. But how do you know who is best suited to handle (and finish) certain tasks? It's simple.

Spend a few minutes determining a few strengths and weaknesses of each member. Simply ask each member what are three of their strengths that would benefit the organization. Also ask each member what are three of their weaknesses. Delegate tasks to any members who are strongest in certain areas that will relate to that task.

Quick Action Step

List each group member and three of their strengths and three of their weaknesses.

GREAT

LEADER

One of your primary roles as a student leader is to give the organization direction. Direction comes from setting goals. Not having goals is similar to trying to drive a car to a destination you've never visited, but not having a roadmap to follow. Can you get there? Possibly. But you may get lost several times along the journey, resulting in anxiety and frustration. The same holds true for your organization. You need to have goals; your roadmap. Follow this simple formula for setting goals. Always set **S.M.A.R.T.** goals:

Specific
Measurable
Attainable
Realistic
Time Limit

Quick Action Step

Practice setting a **S.M.A.R.T** goal by filling in the blanks.

S:______________________________________

(Be *specific* on what you want to achieve)

M:______________________________________

(Make sure to *measure* your progress)

A:______________________________________

(Goals have to be *attainable* for the group)

R:______________________________________

(Goals have to be *realistic* to the group)

T:______________________________________

(Goals need to have a *time limit*/deadline)

GREAT

LEADER

11

Be a Good Listener

It's amazing what you can learn from group members if you will simply listen. Too many student leaders believe they know it all because they're the leader. Being a leader doesn't mean you know it all, it just means that you hold the position. Group members will usually inform you as to what motivates them...or what's working and why...or what's not working and why...or how the group can improve, etc. But it's up to you to listen! Besides, no group member will rally behind a leader who isn't open to the input of the members.

Quick Action Step

List two scenarios in which certain group members were trying to suggest ideas, but you weren't open to listening to their ideas. Then, list why you didn't listen. Approach those members immediately, apologize and ask them to restate their ideas.

GREAT

LEADER

12

Take Responsibility for Your Mistakes

There will be times in your role as a student leader when you will make mistakes. You may make the wrong decision relating to a particular situation. You may delegate tasks to certain group members who aren't best suited for handling and finishing them. You may indirectly embarrass a group member by publicly criticizing them.

Mistakes are understandable as we all make them. Not taking responsibility for mistakes is not. Not taking responsibility for mistakes will lead to a lack of trust from group members.

Quick Action Step

Can you think of any situation when you made a mistake but didn't take responsibility for it?

(Circle Answer)

Yes or No

If you circled "yes," list one or two actions you WILL immediately take to NOW take responsibility for that mistake. (Hint: you may need to start by telling your group members, apologizing, and asking for their forgiveness).

GREAT

LEADER

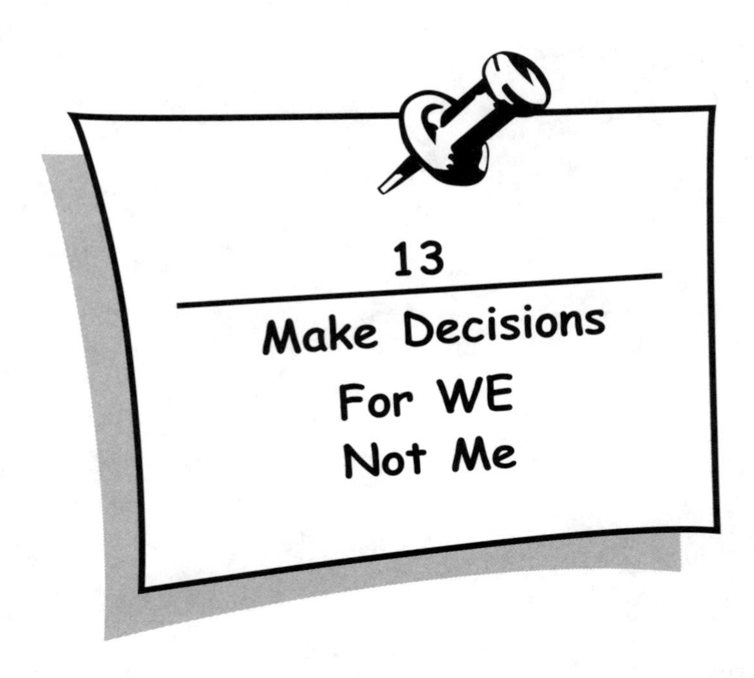

13

Make Decisions For WE Not Me

Decisions are a critical part of being a leader. One decision can make or break the enthusiasm, momentum and direction of your organization.

It's easy to fall into the trap of making decisions more beneficial to you than your organization. Don't allow this to happen. Focus on making decisions that will be in the best interest of the organization.

Quick Action Step

List a few situations where you are faced with a major group decision. Ask yourself if the decision you are contemplating will be more beneficial to yourself or the group. If you find that you'll benefit from the decision more than the group, then you may need to rethink your decision.

GREAT

LEADER

14

Learn How to Effectively Manage Your Time

As a student, you are busy with attending classes, studying for exams, working on projects, being a member of organizations and having a social life. Now, add the role of being a student leader and one thing is for sure: your time is very limited! Make it a point to learn as mush as you can about how to effectively manage your time. Read a book on time management skills, ask for advice from your advisor, and get a day planner to organize your schedule. Effective time management is essential for becoming a more effective and productive leader.

Quick Action Step

Your two time management homework assignments:

1. Go to a bookstore and purchase a book on time management and a day planner to organize your schedule.

2. Set an appointment with your advisor to discuss tips for how to better manage your time. List the appointment date and time here.

My appointment date and time is:

____

GREAT

LEADER

15

Create a Fun Environment

Take time to evaluate the environment of your organization. Is it friendly or hostile? Is it positive or negative? Is it encouraging or discouraging? Is it filled with laughter or tension?

Students seldom desire to be actively involved in an organization if they're not having a fun and enjoyable experience. When students are having fun in an organization, they will be more creative, will develop better ideas and will produce better results.

Quick Action Step

List five or more ways YOU can create a more fun and enjoyable environment for your organization.

GREAT

LEADER

Too many student leaders mistakenly believe that leadership is about having power over those they are leading. They try to lead by commanding and demanding. Trying to lead group members with this method is sure to lead your group toward failure.

Great student leaders understand that their primary role is to **"empower"** group members to work together, struggle together and achieve together as a **TEAM**.

TEAM = **T**ogether **E**veryone **A**chieves **M**ore

Quick Action Step

List three ways you may have been leading with power. Then list three ways you can better lead to "**empower**."

GREAT

LEADER

17

Build Trust By Always Doing the Right Thing

Here's a simple formula for building trust with group members: Always do the right thing! It sounds simple because it is. When faced with a decision, ask yourself, *Is this the right thing to do?* If your answer is no, then don't do it. It only takes you not doing the right thing, once, to lose the trust of your group members forever.

Quick Action Step

Be honest with yourself. List a time when you didn't do the right thing. Think about the situation. Why do you think you didn't do the right thing? What can you learn from it?

GREAT

LEADER

18

Do Your Best

Strive to do your best in every situation. We always seem to appreciate our efforts most when we know in our hearts that we've done the absolute best we could possibly do. And your group members will appreciate that about you as well. As long as you are honestly doing your very best in every situation...that's all anyone can ever ask of you. And you know when you're not putting forth your best effort because you just don't feel good about your effort. Focus on always doing the best you can possibly do as a student leader.

Quick Action Step

List a few simple ways you can consistently demonstrate that you are doing your best.

GREAT

LEADER

19

Allow Group Members to Make Mistakes

When I'm giving a motivational leadership talk to a group of student leaders, I will usually say,

"Adversity is the best university because from adversity we're taught lessons if we only allow our eyes and ears to catch the message and we allow ourselves to learn from it!"

Many leaders believe that mistakes are bad. Actually, mistakes can be one of the best teachers. Encourage your group members to look for the lesson in their mistakes.

Quick Action Step

List three recent mistakes you've made as a leader. What can you learn from these mistakes?

GREAT

LEADER

20

Be Enthusiastic

There's an old saying:

"Enthusiasm Is Contagious!"

Don't expect your group members to be enthusiastic about being a member of your organization or about working on a group project if YOU (the leader) aren't enthusiastic.

Quick Action Step

List three ways YOU can demonstrate your enthusiasm to group members.

GREAT

LEADER

Some leaders have a tendency to single out certain group members and make them be perceived as being more important to the organization than the other members. Don't do that! It will only create apprehension and tension within the organization.

Create an understanding that all members are equally valued and appreciated and that each group member plays an important part for the success of the organization.

Quick Action Step

List three ways YOU can immediately convey that ALL group members are valued and appreciated.

GREAT

LEADER

22

Praise Publicly

A great way to build momentum and create excitement within your organization is to praise a group member publicly, meaning in front of other group members. When other group members see and hear a fellow group member being praised it makes them want to perform better so they, too, can receive the same recognition in front of other members. Simply praising a good deed or action in front of other group members will begin to promote an environment where members begin to publicly praise each other.

Quick Action Step

List two group members who you could have praised publicly for a recent good deed or action, but didn't. Now go do it!

GREAT

LEADER

Where as you should strive to praise publicly, you should strive to criticize privately, away from other group members. Criticizing a group member in front of other group members will do two things:

(1) Embarrass the member you're criticizing in front of the other group members.

(2) Make those who see and hear you publicly criticizing (and embarrassing) a fellow group to not do their best for the fear of making mistakes and receiving the same embarrassment.

Quick Action Step

List a recent experience when you were criticized in front of others. How did it make you feel? Group members will feel the same way if you publicly criticize them in front of group members.

GREAT

LEADER

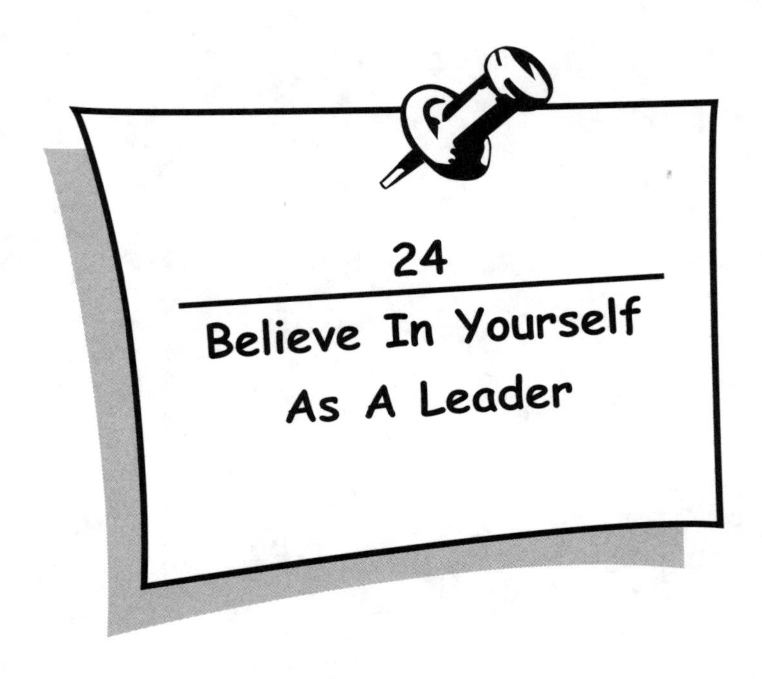

24

Believe In Yourself As A Leader

As a student leader, you may encounter people who tell you that you will not succeed as a leader. You may encounter people who tell you that you don't have the ability to be a great student leader. And you may encounter people who just don't believe in you and your abilities.

SO WHAT!

It ONLY matters if YOU believe in yourself and your abilities. You will succeed as a leader if YOU (and only you) believe that YOU WILL SUCCEED!

Quick Action Step

List a recent situation when you listened to someone who said you couldn't accomplish a goal as a leader. Now, change your thinking and BELIEVE IN YOURSELF!

GREAT

LEADER

25

Focus On Your Strengths

Many student leaders focus on their weaknesses rather than their strengths. Therefore, they minimize their potential by creating incorrect images of themselves.

Assess which of your personal strengths make you a great student leader then determine how you can use those strengths to your advantage when leading others.

Quick Action Step

List three of your strengths that make YOU a Great Student Leader.

GREAT

LEADER

26

Prioritize Using the A-B-C Format

One of your tasks as a student leader will be juggling, or handling, various activities for your organization. The easiest way to do this is by prioritizing. Try the simple **"A-B-C Format."** List all of the activities on a sheet of paper then label each one with either an A, B or C.

A = Most important and must be done immediately!

B = Fairly important but doesn't need to be done until the "A's" are completed.

C = Least important and can wait until all of the "A's" and "B's" are completed.

Quick Action Step

List all of your group activities then prioritize them in the "**A-B-C format.**"

GREAT

LEADER

As a student leader, group members look to you for your creativeness when it comes to solving problems, making decisions and designing a plan to achieve your organizations' objectives.

It's important to consistently active your creative thinking. An easy way to do this is by simply putting yourself in a quiet, relaxing environment and do nothing but "think!" Take 30-minutes to do nothing but focus on the problem, decision or plan. NO distractions—just "think!"

Quick Action Step

Schedule 30-minutes once a week where you will sit in a quiet, relaxing place and do nothing but "think!"

GREAT

LEADER

Keep your advisor informed and involved with the progress of your group. You'll be amazed at the help, support and encouragement you will receive simply by doing this. Your advisor will be able to offer you tips, strategies and ideas for creative problem solving, motivating group members and achieving greater overall success. But, unless YOU make it a priority to keep him/her informed and involved, how will he/she know how to assist you?

Quick Action Step

Make a progress report for your organization. Call your advisor and schedule an appointment to discuss it.

GREAT

LEADER

As a student leader, you will be in a position to hear many fine guest speakers at your school or at conferences. There's a reason why they have been asked (and probably paid) to speak. Because of their accomplishments and of their ability to convey a helpful message. Why wouldn't you want to know someone like that? Seek out the speaker after the presentation, introduce yourself, ask for a business card, then stay in touch! You'll be amazed at how easy it is to do so. Guest speakers are hardly ever approached in this manner. I should know because I've delivered over 1,500 presentations as a guest speaker and I could name three student leaders who have done this...and I'm still in contact with all three of them to this day.

Quick Action Step

Take the following pledge:

I, ____________________________, pledge
(Print Your Name)

to take the initiative to meet every guest

speaker that I hear speak at my school

or at a conference!

____
(Signature)

____
(Date)

GREAT

LEADER

Whether you become a **Great Student Leader** is solely up to you. No one can do it for you. No one can promise or guarantee what level of success you and your organization will achieve. However, by following simple leadership tips, like those outlined in this book, YOU CAN begin to become a **Great Student Leader**. But YOU must take action and begin using the tips.

YOU CAN DO IT -
THE TIME TO START IS NOW!

Quick Action Step

List five tips you have just read that YOU WILL immediately put into action.

www.Malinchak.com

Speaking Engagements

James Malinchak is recognized worldwide as one of the top motivational speakers for students. He was voted College Speaker of the Year by Campus Activities magazine and the Association for the Promotion of Campus Activities (APCA). James has delivered his motivational messages at more than 1,500 youth events, colleges and conferences worldwide.

James is the author of ten books including the top-sellers, *From College to the Real World* and *Teenagers Tips for Success*. He is a Contributing Author to, and serves as an Associate Editor for, the #1 Best-selling book series *Chicken Soup for the Soul®*. James is also a Contributing Editor for *Chicken Soup for the College Soul®* and is published in *Chicken Soup for the Teenage Soul®*.

To Check Speaking Availability, Contact:

JamesMal@aol.com
1-888-793-1196
www.Malinchak.com

James Malinchak

"America's Hottest Young Speaker®"

A few words of Motivation and Inspiration:

"Success Starts With Attitude™!"

"What it takes to be successful is not how much smarts you have,
it's how much HEART you have!"

"Take the 'T' out of can't!"

"It takes TEAMWORK to make your DREAM WORK!"

"Great leaders encourage rather than discourage!"

"Always tell your family how much you love them!"

"When you see the word impossible you should always see
I'M POSSIBLE!"

"Life's not fair or unfair.
Life is life and we need to play the hand we're dealt!"

"Others may help you develop your ability, but you're the
only one who can use it!"

The Ideal Professional Speaker for Your Next Event!

To Schedule James To Speak At Your Event:

1-888-793-1196 • JamesMal@aol.com • www.Malinchak.com